[redacted]

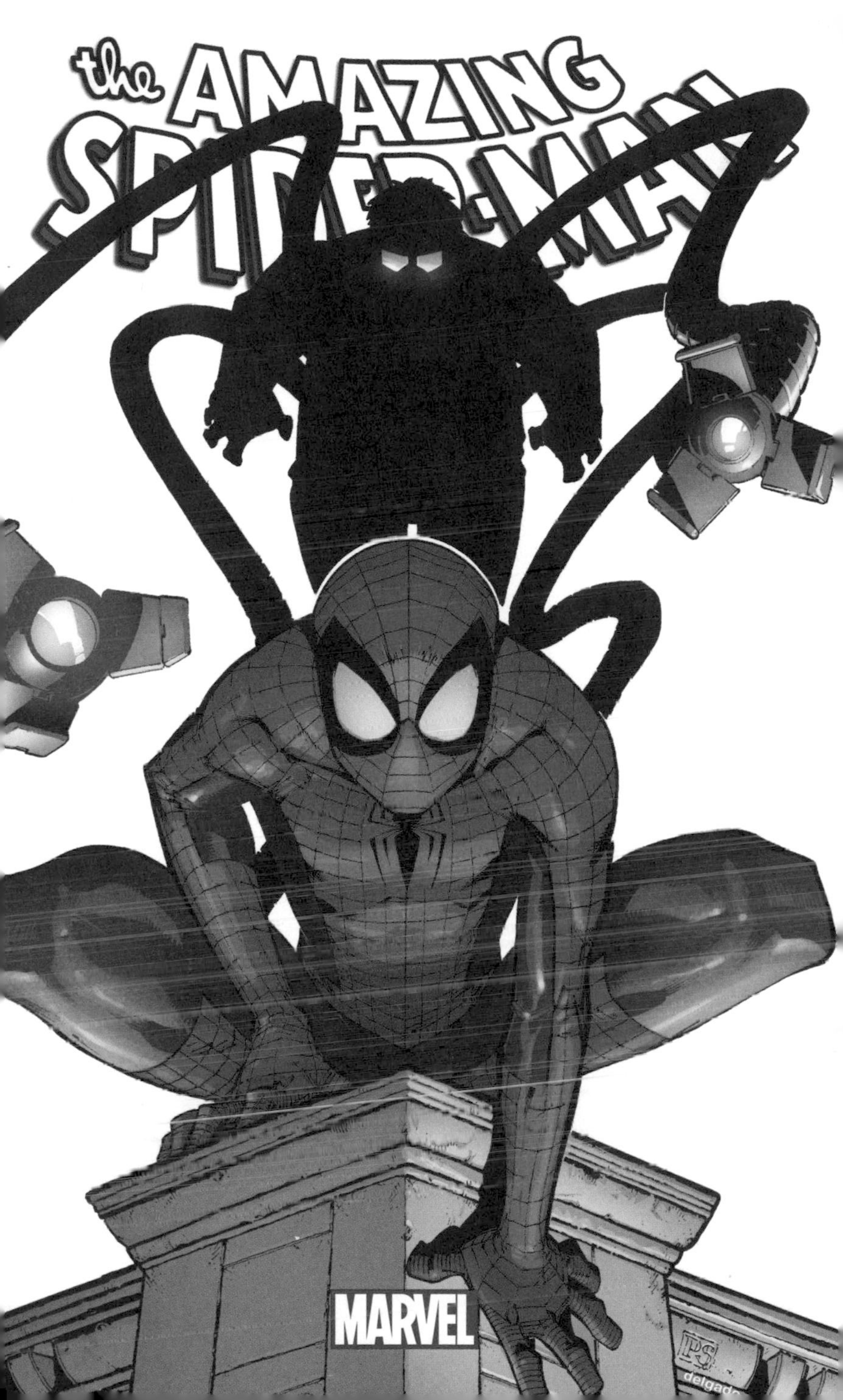
the AMAZING SPIDER-MAN
MARVEL

AMAZING SPIDER-MAN VOL. 3: DR. OCTOPUS YOUNG READERS NOVEL. First printing 2012. ISBN# 978-0-7851-6611-5. Published by MARVEL WORLDWIDE, INC., a subsidiary of MARVEL ENTERTAINMENT, LLC. OFFICE OF PUBLICATION: 135 West 50th Street, New York, NY 10020. Copyright © 2012 Marvel Characters, Inc. All rights reserved. $6.99 per copy in the U.S. and $7.99 in Canada (GST #R127032852); Canadian Agreement #40668537. All characters featured in this issue and the distinctive names and likenesses thereof, and all related indicia are trademarks of Marvel Characters, Inc. No similarity between any of the names, characters, persons, and/or institutions in this magazine with those of any living or dead person or institution is intended, and any such similarity which may exist is purely coincidental. **Printed in the U.S.A.** ALAN FINE, EVP - Office of the President, Marvel Worldwide, Inc. and EVP & CMO Marvel Characters B.V.; DAN BUCKLEY, Publisher & President - Print, Animation & Digital Divisions; JOE QUESADA, Chief Creative Officer; TOM BREVOORT, SVP of Publishing; DAVID BOGART, SVP of Operations & Procurement, Publishing; RUWAN JAYATILLEKE, SVP & Associate Publisher, Publishing; C.B. CEBULSKI, SVP of Creator & Content Development; DAVID GABRIEL, SVP of Publishing Sales & Circulation; MICHAEL PASCIULLO, SVP of Brand Planning & Communications; JIM O'KEEFE, VP of Operations & Logistics; DAN CARR, Executive Director of Publishing Technology; SUSAN CRESPI, Editorial Operations Manager; ALEX MORALES, Publishing Operations Manager; STAN LEE, Chairman Emeritus. For information regarding advertising in Marvel Comics or on Marvel.com, please contact Niza Disla, Director of Marvel Partnerships, at ndisla@marvel.com. For Marvel subscription inquiries, please call 800-217-9158. **Manufactured between 8/13/2012 and 9/17/2012 by SHERIDAN BOOKS, INC., CHELSEA, MI, USA.**

10 9 8 7 6 5 4 3 2 1

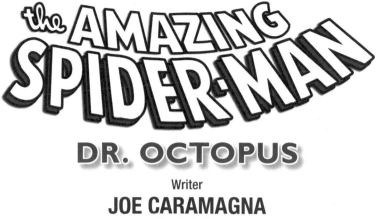

DR. OCTOPUS

Writer
JOE CARAMAGNA
Comic Artist
TIM SEELEY
Colorist
SOTOCOLOR
Letterer
JOE CARAMAGNA
Cover Artists
PATRICK SCHERBERGER with **EDGAR DELGADO**
Spot Illustrations
SCOTT KOBLISH with **SOTOCOLOR**
and **PAUL RYAN, JOHN ROMITA SR., JOHN ROMITA JR. & DAMION SCOTT**
Comic Editor
JORDAN D. WHITE
Prose Editor
CORY LEVINE
Special Thanks To **MIKE FICHERA & TOM SMITH**

Assistant Editors: Alex Starbuck & Nelson Ribeiro
Editors, Special Projects: Jennifer Grünwald & Mark D. Beazley
Senior Editor, Special Projects: Jeff Youngquist
Senior Vice President of Sales: David Gabriel
Associate Publisher & SVP of Print, Animation and Digital Media: Ruwan Jayatilleke
SVP of Brand Planning & Communications: Michael Pasciullo
Book Design: Marie Drion & Joe Frontirre
Editor In Chief: Axel Alonso
Chief Creative Officer: Joe Quesada
Publisher: Dan Buckley
Executive Producer: Alan Fine

SPIDER-MAN

The former professional wrestler turned super hero learned the hard way that with great power must come great responsibility. To make up for his past mistakes, he has vowed to protect New York City from all those who wish to do harm.

PETER PARKER

Raised from childhood by his Uncle Ben and Aunt May, he always dreamed of becoming a scientist like his late father. But after a lab accident — and a radioactive spider bite — granted him special powers, he discovered his true calling.

UNCLE BEN

As Peter's father figure, Uncle Ben has taught him many life lessons. But the most important one of all is that "with great power, there must also come great responsibility."

AUNT MAY

After the death of Peter's parents, May Parker and her husband, Ben, raised their nephew as if he were their own child.

BEN URICH

Ben Urich is the eyes and ears of New York City for *The Daily Bugle*. In an ever-changing world where sensationalism rules, he just wants to tell the whole truth and nothing but.

J. JONAH JAMESON

The publisher of *The Daily Bugle* brings attention to his floundering newspaper by going after New York City's beloved costumed vigilante.

CAPTAIN STACY

A veteran of the police department, Captain Stacy keeps law and order in New York City.

THE VULTURE

Adrian Toomes spent his life as an engineer, but never felt appreciated by his employers. After he was fired, he decided to use his greatest invention, the Vulture harness, to gain the respect he felt he always deserved.

SANDMAN

While on the run from the police, a chemical accident left criminal Flint Marko with the ability to turn his body into sand.

DOCTOR OCTOPUS

Dr. Otto Octavius is a world-renowned, yet accident-prone, nuclear physicist. After one accident too many left him melded to a set of four mechanical arms, he became Spider-Man's most formidable super villain!

GREEN GOBLIN

Norman Osborn is a military contractor who was tasked with developing a super-soldier serum. But aside from extraordinary abilities, his flawed formula also brings out his devilish dark side!

KRAVEN THE HUNTER

After conquering the fiercest animals in all the jungles of Africa, the hunter Sergei Kravinoff set his sights on the most elusive game of them all: the Amazing Spider-Man!

THE LIZARD

Dr. Curt Connors developed a serum to replicate a lizard's ability to regenerate limbs in humans. But when he tested it on himself, he got more than he bargained for!

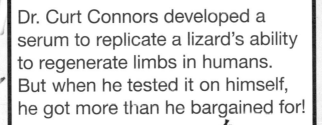

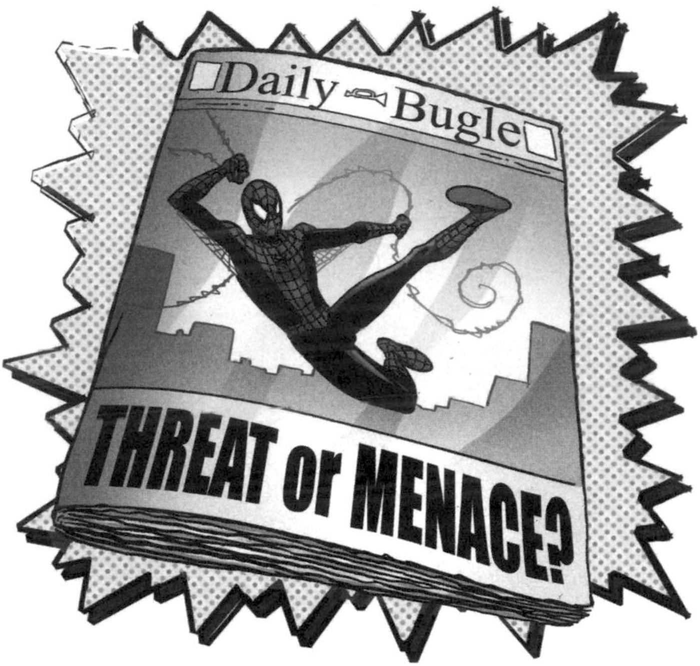
Daily Bugle
THREAT or MENACE?

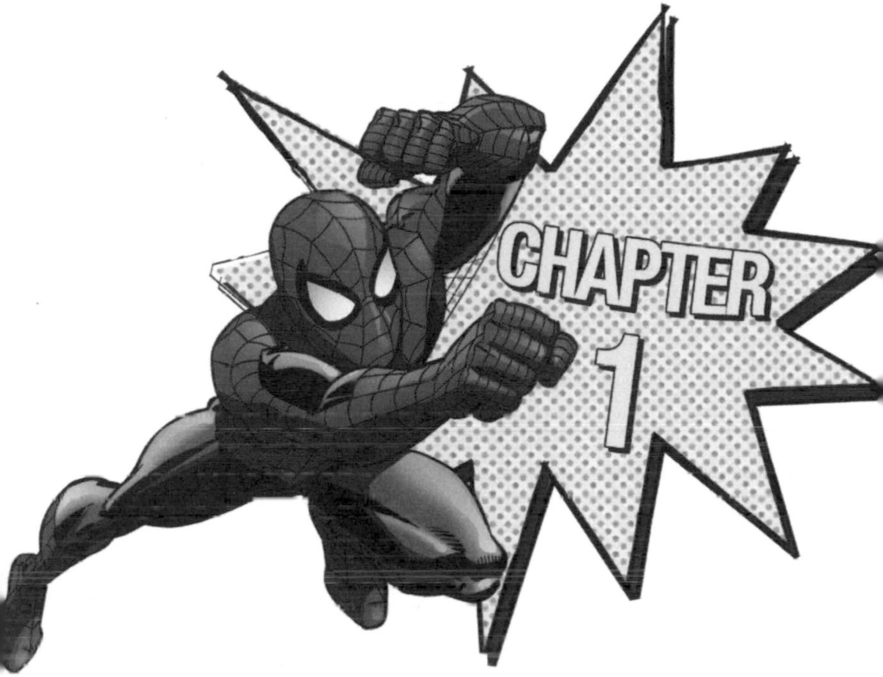
CHAPTER
1

"BUZZ BUZZ BUZZ BUZZ!"

There was a time when the morning sun was a welcome sight to Peter Parker. It meant the start of a new day at Midtown High, where the next chapter of his science textbook was waiting to be explored. But that was *then*.

A few weeks ago, Peter went on a class trip to Empire State University's science labs, where he was bitten by a radioactive spider and somehow gained its proportional abilities! Ever since that fateful day, those powers have continued to strengthen. At first, he could leap thirty feet into the air. Now, he could leap *one hundred* and thirty! He *was* able to lift five hundred pounds over his head, but now he could lift a *two-ton* car. Even his eyesight had gotten stronger, and he no longer needed the glasses he had worn since third grade. Every day, Peter wondered what new abilities he would develop next.

Now, with a new name and costume, Peter Parker patrols New York City as the AMAZING SPIDER-MAN! And because he is much stronger and faster than any police officer, criminals everywhere are coming up with new and clever ways to do their evil deeds.

Unfortunately for Peter, a promising high-school student, most of those evil deeds happened at night, well past his bedtime.

"BUZZ BUZZ BUZZ BUZZ," the alarm clock shouted.

Peter pulled his pillow down over his ears and wished the noise would stop. Unfortunately, that's one power he hadn't developed yet. He finally threw his arms up in surrender and switched the alarm to radio mode to listen to the news of the day — a habit he picked up since he started fighting crime as Spider-Man. Then, he pulled some clothes from his dresser drawer and dragged his weary bones into the hallway. On his way to the shower, he smelled something coming from the kitchen — something he hadn't smelled in a long time.

Peter's Uncle Ben was a self-proclaimed wheat cakes connoisseur who claimed to have tried the wheat cakes in every diner across the country. Nobody knew whether this was true, of course, because Uncle Ben liked to tell stories. Peter couldn't ever remember a time when his uncle had even left the state of New

York. But according to Ben, Aunt May's wheat cakes were the best he'd ever tasted. Whenever he asked her how she got her wheat cakes to taste so good, Aunt May joked it was a government secret — and that if she told, she'd go to prison for life. He vowed he'd discover her recipe. One day, he hid behind the kitchen door to try to catch her in the act! But of course she saw him, because nobody could ever fool Aunt May!

Ever since he passed away, Aunt May hadn't made her special breakfast because she was afraid it would remind her of her late husband. And Peter had been avoiding her, probably for the same reason she avoided the wheat cakes. He always had some excuse for staying out until after she had gone to bed and rushing out in the morning before breakfast. But she decided enough time had passed that they were ready to be normal again — whatever "normal" meant now that it was just the two of them. As she mixed the secret ingredients together in a bowl, she found out she was right: She did

think about Uncle Ben. But instead of crying, she smiled.

When Aunt May ladled the batter into the skillet, that old, familiar smell of family filled the kitchen. She knew once the aroma reached his nose, Peter would come along any minute, and maybe she'd actually see him smile for the first time in months. While she waited, she hummed loudly to herself as the morning news played on the television behind her.

"— all in all, a beautiful day that's been a long time coming," the newsman said. "Enjoy it, New York! Savannah?"

"Thanks, Chuck. We have some breaking news out of Empire State University, where eyewitnesses on the ground are reporting that a large mechanical object — a giant robot —

is on a rampage, destroying everything in its path.

"At this point, we're not sure who is responsible for it or where it came from, but the ESU science campus has seen its share of disasters lately —"

A loud *THUD!* came from Peter's bedroom, right above Aunt May's head, immediately followed by hurried footsteps that traveled from his bedroom, down the stairs, past the kitchen, through the living room and toward the front door.

"WAIT!" Aunt May chased after Peter with a skillet of wheat cakes still in her hand, but he was already halfway out the door.

"Sorry, Aunt May," he shouted over his shoulder. "I'm...uh, late for class!"

Aunt May was so sure the wheat cakes would make this morning different. Without thinking, she cupped her hand around her mouth and shouted, "Well, don't forget about dinner, then. I'm making your favorite!" She hadn't actually planned anything for dinner, but she wasn't about to let her nephew off the hook so easily.

She closed the door and looked down at the wheatcakes in her skillet, raw on the top, but blackening at the edges. She turned to throw them away, when she noticed Peter's backpack leaning against the wall. He ran off so quickly he left it behind! She snapped open the door and shouted down the stairs, "Peter, wait! You forgot your school books!"

But he was long gone. And he wasn't on his way to class.

After a quick change in the alley, Spider-Man swung swiftly between the skyscrapers on his way to the Empire State University campus. Running toward a rampaging killer robot

was the last thing Peter wanted to be doing, even with the proportional powers of a spider. Especially on a morning like this when he didn't have enough sleep and his head was pounding like it was hatching a baby dinosaur. And it was only getting worse.

When he arrived, the police were already there. Spider-Man could always pick Captain Stacy out of the crowd — he stood just a little bit taller than the other two hundred officers at the scene. Some of them set up a perimeter a safe distance away, while the others guided frightened college students to safety.

And then Spidey saw it. Crawling

out from behind the auditorium
toward the science building was a
fifty-foot-tall, eight-legged mechanical
monster! It moved like a spider — a
large, round body walking on long
metal arms. In the center of its body
was a large, glowing orange "eye" that

surveyed the scene menacingly. Spider-Man swung over Captain Stacy's head, bounced off the hood of a police car and launched himself toward the mechanical beast. "Hey, fellas," he said to the cops.

"Hey," Officer Kowalski shouted. "It's that spider guy!"

"I have to get his autograph for my kid," said Officer Romita.

But Captain Stacy snarled. For weeks now, Spider-Man had been showing up the NYPD by stopping all of the bad guys they couldn't. He wasn't about to let him hog all the glory for this one, too. "Well, what are you waiting for?" he said to his men. "Let's get this monster!"

Spider-Man landed on the robot's back and knocked politely on its metal hide to get its attention. "Really? Of all the creatures in the world, you have to look like a *spider*?" he said. "In case you haven't noticed, that motif's already taken. But since I can't afford an attorney, I'm afraid we'll have to settle this out of court." The spider-bot raised one of its mechanical arms, scooped the wall-crawler up in its claw

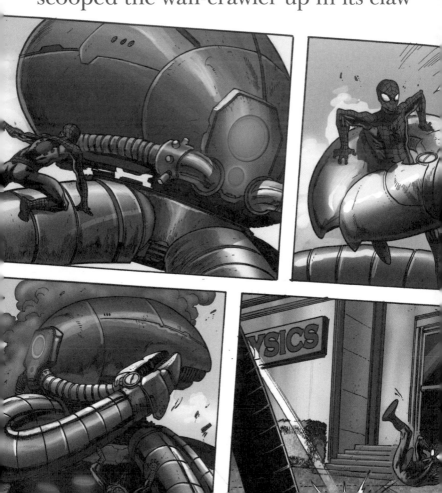

and — with a sharp flick — sent him flying away like a bug.

"Hey, you can't do that to Spider-Man!" Officer Romita called out. He stepped in front of the robot with his gun drawn and fired three shots at its metal body, but the bullets just bounced off! The spider-bot's orange eye rotated in the direction of the officer and glowed to a red. The spider-bot raised a giant arm that had a sledgehammer-shaped knob at the end of it and prepared to strike!

With a sudden THWIP! of his web-shooter, Spider-Man swung in between them and grabbed Officer Romita by the belt buckle. He lifted him out of harm's way just before the heavy arm slammed down and split the sidewalk in half right where the officer had been standing! Spider-Man set him down in a safe place and turned to face the robot again. The robot raised his sledgehammer arm, and suddenly Peter felt it again — the sharp pain that pounded at his ears from the inside. He squeezed his head between his hands and collapsed to the ground, just barely out of the way of the spider-bot's blow, which slammed into the brick wall behind him.

Spider-Man rolled away, as the robot continued to pound at the

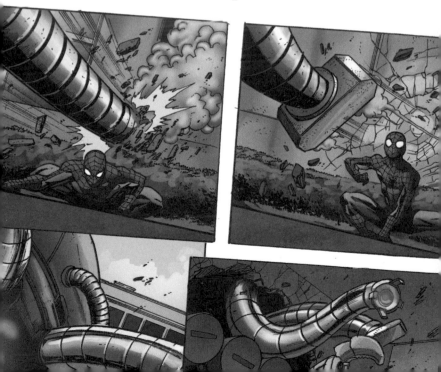

bricks of the science building, clearing out a large portion of the wall. Then, it raised another arm with a drill at the end of it and began to bore a hole. As his headache cleared, Spider-Man noticed the robot wasn't a weapon of mass destruction. It was a tool — a giant Swiss Army Knife — that was here for a different, specific purpose.

"What is it doing?" Officer Kowalski asked. Captain Stacy raised his hand to silence him, waiting for the robot to make its next move. The spider-bot reached into the building with its claws and sorted through the laboratory equipment inside, and a hatch opened up on the top of its body. As it found what it was looking for, it tossed the selected scientific instruments into its body.

"It's robbing the lab," the surprised Captain Stacy said.

When it was done, the mechanical spider retracted its arms and closed its lid. Its eye rotated to the other side of its body as it crawled away. "Oh, come on now! Didn't your giant-mechanical-killer-spider-robot mother ever teach you it's not nice to steal?" Spider-Man pressed the button on the web-shooters he wore on his wrists and wrapped the robot's long legs up

in webs to keep it from getting away, but the legs tore them apart with their powerful strides. Spider-Man jumped up the robot's body and tapped it on the eye to get its attention. "Excuse me, spider-copycat, I'm talking to you." The spider-bot stopped, and its eye glowed red again. It was a really bad time for Spider-Man's headache to come back, but he was able to keep his wits about him and jump out of the way just as the robot fired a laser beam from its eye that scorched a deep hole in the ground!

"Everybody back!" Captain Stacy shouted, waving his arms toward the crowd.

"Hey! That's cheating!" Spider-Man yelled, sitting on the ground below. "Spiders don't have laser beams!"

With that, the spider-bot turned away from Spider-Man and stood up

tall. A soft rumbling sound came from its body and grew into a loud roar as flames burst from its underbelly and launched it into the air. In an instant, it was out of sight.

"You're under arrest!" Captain Stacy shouted at Spider-Man when he climbed to his feet.

"Huh?! For what?!"

"Interfering with police business, for one thing. And you might not think much of us guys in uniform, but we are smart enough to notice that thing had eight arms. Like a spider!"

"You think *I* planned this?"

"Captain," a voice called from the side. "He...he saved my life," Officer Romita said, wiping the dirt from the knees of his uniform.

Captain Stacy looked back at Spider-Man and poked him in the chest. "I'll give you a ten-second head start. Then I'm bringing you in." Without another word, Spider-Man swung away, knowing Captain Stacy could never keep up with him.

But it didn't matter. Captain Stacy never followed.

CHAPTER
2

"Isn't it obvious, Parker? That robot's got the wall-crawling menace's sticky fingers all over it!"

At one time, *The Daily Bugle* had been the city's most trusted newspaper, but it had lost many of its readers to the shameless new tabloids in recent years. Publisher J. Jonah Jameson had decided the best way for the paper to attract new readers was to stand out from its competitors by making an enemy of the city's new hero, Spider-Man. The plan had been working thanks to Jonah's hotshot young photographer, Peter Parker, who had a knack for getting the best pictures of the web-slinger, which gave the newspaper added credibility. Because Peter was just a teenager, Jonah kept his identity secret, but little did Jonah know his young employee *was* Spider-Man and

used his uncle's old camera with a
self-timer to photograph himself in
action. Peter hated the way Jameson
used his pictures, but he put up with
it because not only did the checks
help pay Aunt May's rent, but the
newsroom was also the place to go to
get real information.

"Why aren't you in school?" Jonah
asked.

"I was there! I saw it with my own
eyes! Spider-Man did everything he
could to stop it."

"Is that so? Did you get me any
pictures of it?"

Peter looked down at his shoes and shuffled his feet. "Well…" he said, "I forgot my camera in my backpack at home, and —"

Before he could finish his sentence, Jonah walked into his office and slammed the door behind him. *So much for gathering information*, Peter thought.

"So *you're* the one!" a voice shouted out.

Peter turned to see a middle-aged reporter, tall and slender, cleaning his eyeglasses against his tie. "You're the mystery photographer who gets us all those front-page shots of Spider-Man. What did Jonah call you? Parker?"

Peter looked around to make sure no one else was listening. Nobody knew he was Jonah's anonymous photographer, not even Aunt May. If she ever found out he was chasing Spider-Man around town for pictures, she'd probably ground him for life.

"Don't worry, kid, your secret's safe

with me. I started here when I was underage, too.

"My name's Urich. Ben Urich. I'm the one covering the spider-bot story."

Peter looked at his outstretched hand, but wouldn't shake it. *Urich.* He knew the name, and he wasn't happy. "Wait, you're the writer who called Spider-Man a 'terrorist'?"

Ben laughed loudly. "I just write the stories, kid, not the headlines.

"I know Spider-Man's a hero. No matter what Jonah or Captain Stacy or anyone else says about him, he keeps showing up to do what's right without getting discouraged. We could use some more people like that in this city."

"I agree," Peter said,

smiling widely. He stuck out his hand and gave Urich a proper shake this time. "I'm Peter Parker, Mr. Urich. Nice to meet you."

"Likewise. And you know what? I think you're right. Spider-Man had nothing to do with that spider-bot."

"GREAT! Now how do we convince Mr. Jameson?" Peter asked.

Urich laughed again. "Jonah's going to be Jonah — he's going to believe whatever sells the most newspapers, regardless of what his brain tells him."

"Do *you* know where the spider-bot went?" Peter wondered.

"It took off so fast nobody could track it."

"No eyewitnesses?"

"They're all over the map. People think they see all sorts of things they don't really see," Urich said.

"So how do we find out who's behind it all?"

"Well, you're a journalist, Peter. Consider the facts."

A *journalist!* Peter liked the sound of that!

"What did the spider-bot want?" asked Urich.

"Um...to steal some lab equipment?" Peter guessed.

"Not just any lab equipment, equipment from Otto Octavius' lab that's been sealed since his latest accident a few months back," said Urich. Peter had heard of Dr. Otto Octavius from his science journals. He was brilliant in his day, but had grown careless and erratic.

"His latest accident put him in the hospital, and the university got cold feet and cut off his funding," Urich explained.

"What was he working on?"

"I bet whoever sent that spider-bot knows. But Octavius kept his research a secret, even from the university. They didn't care, though. His presence on campus brought a lot of publicity...and donations. They hoped he'd have something big to show them in the end."

"Why doesn't someone just ask Dr. Octavius what he was making?"

"If he's at his last known address, he's not answering his phone. And it'll take the cops a while to get a search warrant. But believe me, I'd love to be a fly on his wall. It would answer a lot of questions."

Urich excused himself to make some more calls, hoping to find a clue on the other end. Peter wished he were a fly on Octavius' wall, too. But he'd have to settle for being the next best thing: a spider.

If you asked Spider-Man, he'd admit it wasn't one of his proudest moments. What Ben Urich said was true: Octavius wasn't answering his phone, and so Spider-Man climbed up to the roof, into the exhaust pipe, and through the heating ducts until he found the right apartment.

By the time Spider-Man popped open the vent and crawled out onto the ceiling, his headache had returned. *Not now,* Peter thought, *it always comes at the worst times.* The main room was large, without much furniture, which made the laser-beam security system that protected it so diligently seem a bit excessive. Either there was more here than met the eye, or Otto Octavius suffered from severe paranoia. Probably both.

Spider-Man noticed what might have been a broom closet on the other side of the room. Normally, that wasn't the kind of thing that would rouse suspicion, but this one was a steel door with four key locks in a line above the knob. Obviously, Dr. Octavius didn't want nosy visitors at his next party to stumble upon the things in that room, but most nosy visitors wouldn't be able to rip the door from the wall the way Spider-Man could. And he did! With all his might, he pulled until the locks shattered to pieces. His headache was growing stronger now and he heard ringing in his ears, but he couldn't let that stop him after getting so far.

He flipped on the light and gasped when it revealed the room's secrets: stacks of boxes, file cabinets, metal drums, strange bags and containers — all with large stickers on them

warning of radioactive materials. Spider-Man didn't know much about this building, but he guessed most tenants' associations frowned upon storing radioactive materials in your apartment. Spider-Man's lifted the lid of the large, rusty trunk at his feet and saw what looked like a car battery inside, except it was the size of a large suitcase. Spider-Man rubbed his temples to ease the increasingly sharp pain in his head.

Right next to it was a table with blueprints on it that were stamped "Classified" and "Property of Dr. Otto Octavius." *This must be it! His latest experiment!* Spidey flipped through a few pages and realized the device he'd found *was* a battery...containing radioactive material! A *nuclear* battery. There were notes scribbled in the margins that had been crossed out in red marker. Spider-Man tried to make out the notes, but all he could figure out were the words "extreme pressure," "containment structure" and "volatile." Peter Parker was no nuclear physicist, but it looked to him like Octavius had created a small nuclear reactor — and a powerful one at that. But it was a work in progress, for sure.

Spider-Man turned to the next page and saw another technical drawing, this one showing a familiar round-bodied object with eight long tentacles. And each tentacle had a different function with a proper tool at the end of it. It was the spider-bot! No, according to the handwriting underneath, it was an "Octo-Bot." Not a spider, an octopus! Then, he suddenly realized all this stuff had been stolen from Octavius' lab earlier that day.

"Gahh!" The headache hit him hard. It was the worst one yet, bouncing

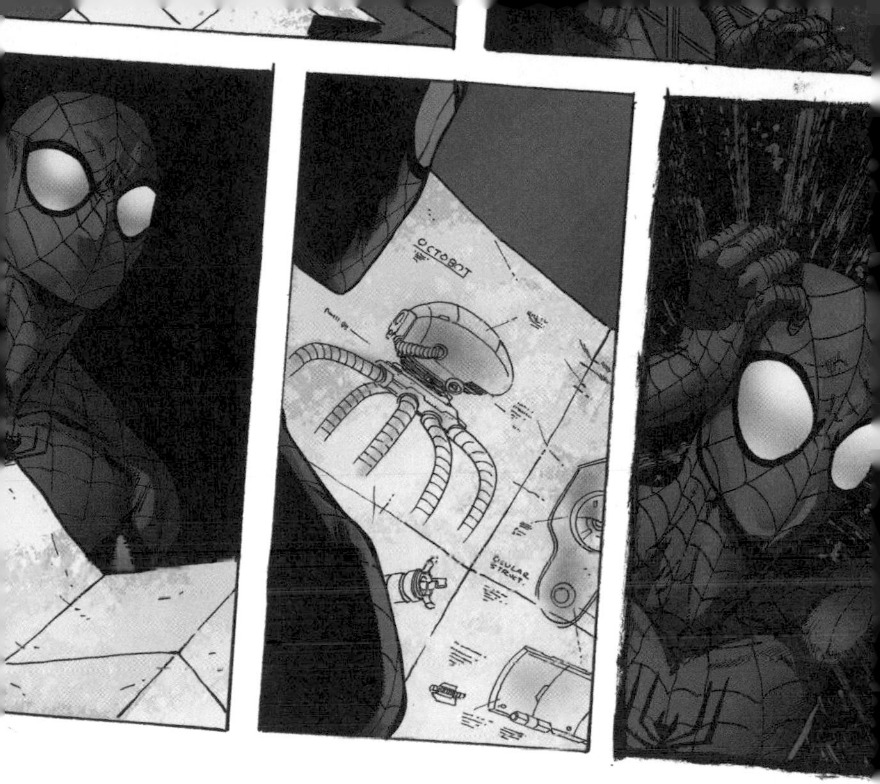
OCTOBOT

around in his skull like a sack full of alarm clocks spinning in a clothes dryer.

Suddenly, steel tentacles reached in through the doorway and pulled him out into the larger room. Spider-Man skidded across the hardwood floor until he crashed into the opposite wall. The tentacles grabbed him around his neck and turned him around. Spider-Man saw the tentacles were attached to the body of his attacker, a middle-aged man with tinted safety goggles and a bowl haircut. Although he looked silly, those tentacles were even stronger than Spider-Man. They responded to the man's mental commands like four extra arms and legs — like an octopus.

It was O*ctavius!*

"Who sent you?!" Octavius asked through gritted teeth.

Spider-Man tried to talk, but the claw on the end of one Octavius' metal arms closed tight around his neck. "Wh-what..." was all he managed to get out.

"Don't feign ignorance! I know you've been following me for years!" Spittle jumped from Octavius' mouth as he shouted. "You're from big oil! Big energy! You're threatened by my creations, and you always have been! You know I am on the verge of

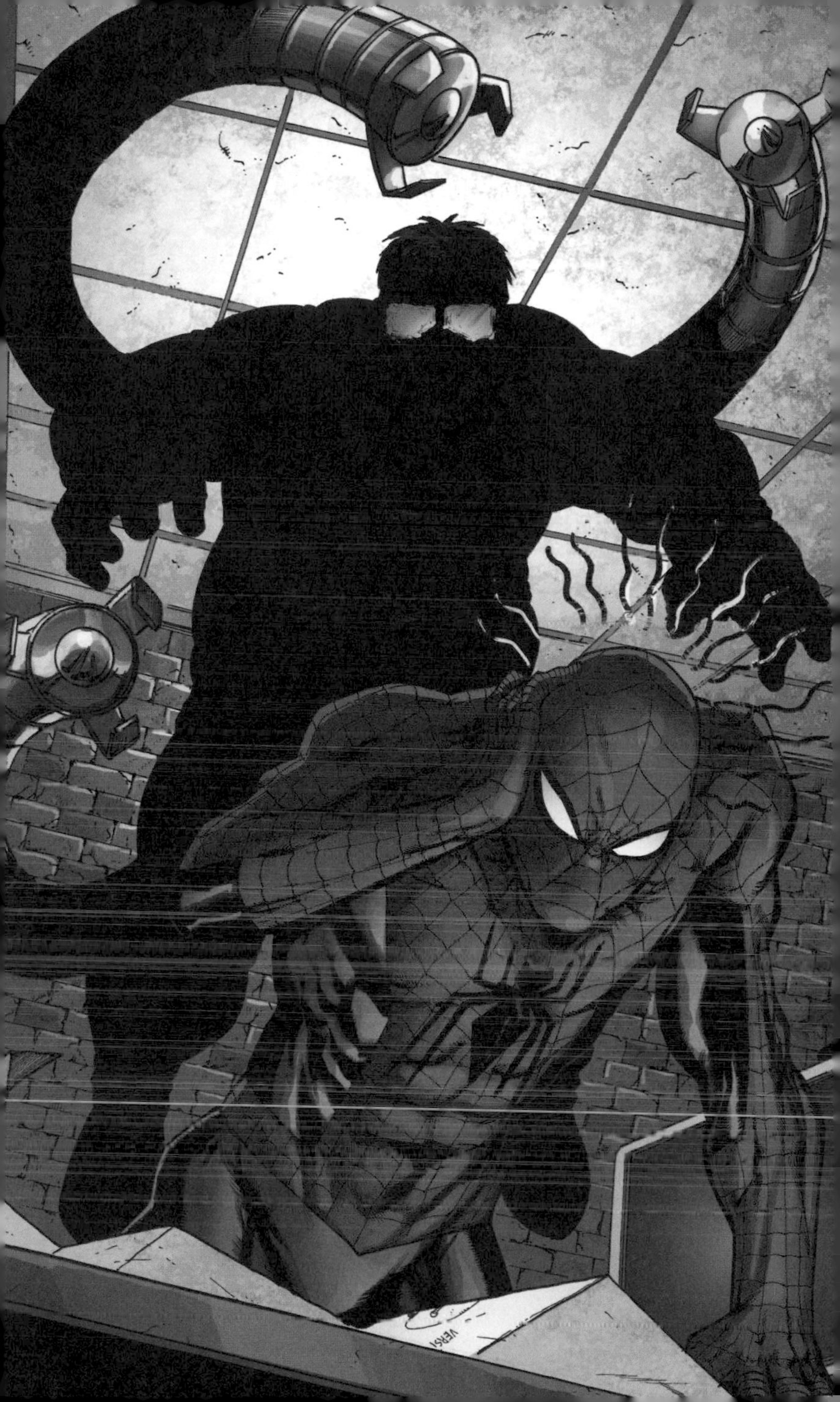

ending your stranglehold on the world economy!"

Spider-Man grabbed the mechanical arm with both hands, but not even his strength could loosen its grip on his throat. "What...are these? Wh-what are you?"

Dr. Octavius growled and pulled him close, so he could look into his eyes through his dark goggles. His lips trembled with rage. "You mean you don't recognize your own handiwork? *You* did this to me!"

Spider-Man had never even met

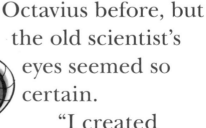

Octavius before, but the old scientist's eyes seemed so certain.

"I created these mechanical arms to handle radioactive

material in my lab," Octavius said. "Your latest attempt to sabotage my experiments caused an explosion of subatomic particles that permanently grafted them to my body.

"But you failed! Do you hear me? I salvaged my work..."

Dr. Octavius lifted Spider-Man off his feet and threw him hard against the brick wall without loosening his grip. Spider-Man's head bounced off it like a rubber ball.

"...and I'M STILL ALIVE!"

Octavius yelled.

In one motion, he peeled Spider-Man off of the wall and slammed him against the one opposite, still holding him by the throat. Spider-Man felt himself slipping away into unconsciousness.

"My nuclear battery will be the innovation of the century!" Octavius continued. "Enough renewable energy to power an entire city in one portable unit. No more oil spills in our fruitful oceans, no more drilling into our precious soil, no more windmills or solar panels to cover our beautiful landscapes.

"No more energy crises!"

Octavius slammed Spider-Man into the wall again. Bricks and mortar cracked under the force of the blow. Stunned, Spider-Man lost control of his legs and arms as he lay limp like a ragdoll.

"When I stole my equipment back from my lab, I didn't expect you to catch up to me so quickly. Your pursuit is relentless. Even I, as strong as I am with my new mechanical arms, can only fight off your kind for so long.

"You've made me realize I'm out of time. If I wait any longer to test it, I could lose it forever. The time to show what I can do is upon us!"

Octavius threw Spider-Man against the wall one last time and his world went dark.

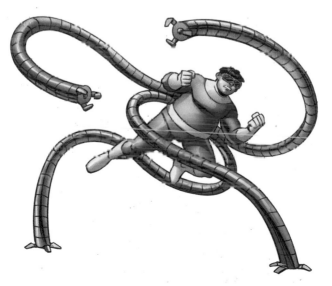

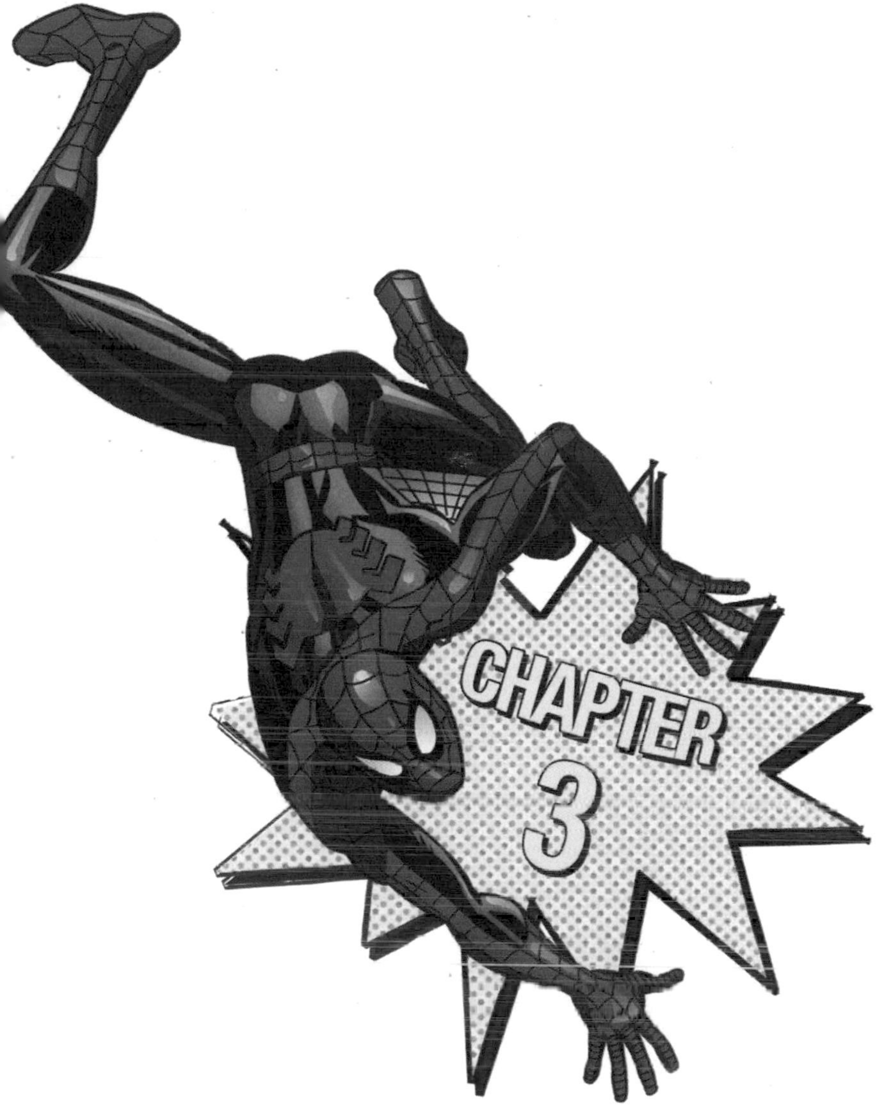
CHAPTER
3

Spaghetti and meatballs? Meatloaf and mashed potatoes? Aunt May had considered the dinner menu all day. Peter liked those dishes well enough — but whenever Uncle Ben came home from a bad day at work, a hearty bowl of her slow-cooked beef stew could always bring good humor to his cheeks. Now that they were going to have their first meal together with Peter as the new man of the house, she hoped it would work its magic on him, as well.

At least that was the plan. But the stew was ready, and Peter still wasn't home. Aunt May decided to try calling the Avenue Club, an upscale eatery in midtown Manhattan. Peter had said his classmate, Liz Allan, had put a good word in with her father, who owned the place, and he had offered to let him work as a dishwasher a few days a week. According to Peter, that's where he usually disappeared to — sometimes not getting home until after Aunt May had gone to bed. She didn't want to pry because he brought in some extra money to help pay the bills, but this was supposed to be a special night.

"Hello, Mr. Allan. This is May Parker, Peter's Aunt.

"Yes, Peter Parker, right. Have you seen him today? He's not home yet and he —"

As Mr. Allan talked into her ear, her face soured. "I beg your pardon, Mr. Allan," she said, "but I'm calling *you* because Peter tells me he's been helping out at the restaurant a few days a week."

Suddenly, her face, and her heart, seemed to fall with

worry. "Oh. I'm sorry. I thought...uh...well, is Liz there? Does she know where Peter might have gone after school?"

Aunt May put her hand to her mouth to hold in her exasperation over what she was hearing. "He wasn't in school today?" She leaned against the kitchen counter to keep from falling down. Tears quickly filled her eyes. Peter had lied to her. All this time. He never worked a single day at the Avenue Club. He didn't show up for school. Where did he get his money? Where did he spend his days?

"No, no, I'm fine, Mr. Allan," she said with a quiver.

"It's just that ever since his Uncle Ben passed, he's been...well, you know how kids are about these kind of things.

"No, that's not necessary, I'll be fine. He'll be fine. Everything will

be fine," she lied. "Sorry to bother you." She threw the phone down and wiped the tears from her cheeks. Peter had made a fool of her, which she never allowed anyone to do. Since Ben passed away, she thought they were in this together — but the truth is he had his own life she wasn't a part of. She turned the burner of the stove off. Peter didn't deserve Ben's beef stew, she thought. She wanted to take the entire pot and throw it in the trash with the wheat cakes.

Peter wasn't sure whether his eyes were open or closed until he felt them blink. The darkness all around him was the darkest dark he'd ever seen. It was unnatural.

Where am I? How did I get here? he wondered.

"Hello?" he called out with a stifled voice.

He went to rub his eyes to get them to work again, but his right arm couldn't move. It was pinned beneath his body. He squirmed onto his back to free it, but his legs wouldn't move with him. Something was holding them down.

With his left hand, he reached out to feel a smooth surface inches away from his face and another one to his side. He tried to unbend his knees, but his feet hit a wall.

Then, suddenly, he remembered where he was.

His heart pounded. He felt the air that was there a minute ago start to run out. After Octavius had beat him up, he had locked Peter in that rusty, old trunk!

He had to get out! Peter pressed his free hand and his knees against the inside of the lid and pressed with all the force he could muster in the tight space. He heard the squeak of a metal lock straining to hold him captive. He pressed harder — so hard his joints ached. His muscles burned. Was it working? He couldn't tell. And just when he thought he had taken his last gulp of air, the padlock shattered into pieces and the lid snapped open. Spider-Man popped out of the box and drank up all the air his lungs could swallow. The air felt cold against his sweat-soaked costume. He was free!

But if he was in the box, what had happened to the nuclear battery that had been in there before him? *That's right!* Peter remembered, *Octavius said he was going to test it.* But that battery gave Peter an uneasy feeling, and the blueprints suggested it wouldn't work. It looked like the casing wouldn't be able to handle the amount of pressure it produced. If the battery exploded, the nuclear blast would destroy most of the city! He had to find Octavius and stop him.

But where to start? Spider-Man swung from the top of Octavius' apartment building on his web line. Down below, the city lights began to sparkle as the sun disappeared behind the horizon. He must have been knocked out for longer than he thought if it was already dusk. As he swung from skyscraper to skyscraper looking for clues, he remembered what Ben Urich taught him: "Consider the facts."

For Dr. Octavius to supply power to the city, he would have to access the power grid through a transmission station. Also, nuclear power requires water, and lots of it. That would mean Octavius had gone to a station on either the Hudson or East River. But which one? If he chose incorrectly, he might not make it back across town in time to stop the mad doctor!

He turned toward the Hudson River when he felt the tingle behind his eyes, which slowly and steadily grew into another powerful headache.

These headaches always came at the worst times: during his fight against the octo-bot, when Octavius had snuck up behind him and now that the city was on the verge of disaster. Considering the facts, Spider-Man realized his headaches came about in times of trouble and the more immediate the danger, the more painful the headache! Since his abilities had progressed so much, could it be possible the headaches were an early warning system of some kind? A "danger sense"? As he headed westward toward the Hudson, the pain in his head grew stronger and screamed louder. He had no choice but to trust it was trying to tell him something. It was his only hope.

By day, commuters, sailors and tourists have a great view of the city from the Hudson River but under the cover of darkness, nobody saw the man with eight arms and legs scale the security fence of the power substation. The station was a forest of shiny metal towers and coils connected by a system of beams and cables that hummed with electrical energy. Dr. Octavius carried the battery in his arms until he found the perfect spot to set it down. He pulled a hose from the side of the battery and dropped into the river. Then, he adjusted his safety goggles and unscrewed the plastic cover from the top of the battery to reveal a series of wires and contacts. After connecting it to a large control panel that plugged into the power grid, he flipped a switch. The battery sparked to life! In a few moments, after it built up enough charge, the city's electrical power supply would transfer from the substation to Dr. Octopus' nuclear battery!

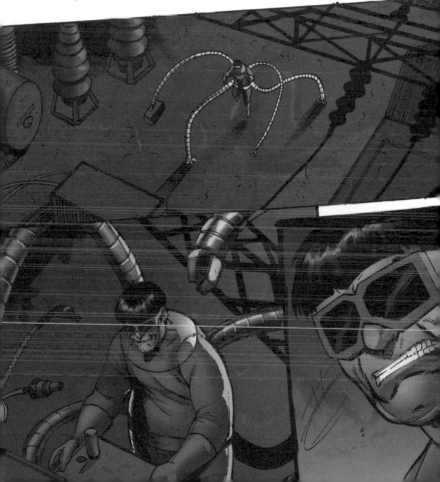

Eager to see the lights on Broadway shine brighter than ever, he turned to leave when suddenly a voice called out, "Hold it, Dr. Octopus!" Spider-Mean leapt from the top of one of the towers and kicked the mad scientist across the face, catching him by surprise. He had learned from their first fight he had to strike first and strike hard before those mechanical tentacles could grab him.

"Raaarrrgh!" Octavius staggered backwards. His mechanical arms were incredibly strong — but without them,

he was just an ordinary man. He wasn't used to getting hit by someone with Spider-Man's strength.

"Dr. Octavius, listen to me," Spider-Man said. "You have to shut down your battery. I saw your blueprints. The container can't handle the kind of pressure —"

Octavius whipped a mechanical arm toward the web-slinger. This time, Spider-Man knew to trust his "danger sense." As soon as he felt the tingle in his head, he ducked quickly out of the way before waiting for his other senses to recognize he was in trouble. Octavius' steel claw jabbed harmlessly at the air. Octavius swung at him with another tentacle — and again, Spider-Man sidestepped it easily.

"You have to trust me," Spider-Man said. "It's not a battery — it's a bomb!"

"You lie!" Octavius screamed. "You

just want it for yourself! To take credit for my work!"

"You're sick, Doc. I promise, I'll do whatever I can to make sure they don't throw you in jail, that they get you the help you need."

Octavius charged at Spider-Man with all his mechanical arms flailing, reaching, grabbing and stabbing all at once. Spider-Man ducked, dodged, jumped and flipped to safety. "Why won't you stay still?" Octavius shouted. He wrapped all four mechanical arms into a steel knot and took a mighty swing at his fidgety foe.

"Sorry," Spider-Man said as he jumped high into the air and out of harm's way. "I've already lost two fights today..."

He landed on Octavius' other side, and Spider-Man pressed

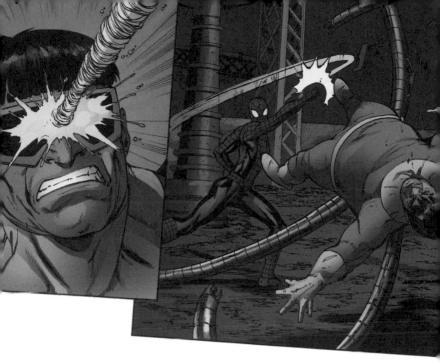

the button on his web-shooter when
the scientist turned around, covering
his safety goggles with sticky goo —
completely blinding him.

"...and I'm not going to lose again!"
Spider-Man launched himself at
Octavius with extraordinary speed and
landed a mighty punch across his chin!

Octavius staggered backwards a
few feet, stumbled and then fell onto
his back. The mechanical arms waved

around in the air wildly before falling all around him with a giant THUD! "Dr. Octopus" was out cold!

But before Peter could catch his breath, his new danger sense came roaring back! He grabbed the sides of his head in pain and turned to see the nuclear battery tremble as the device's low humming grew into an ear-splitting buzz. Peter approached the battery slowly and pulled his Spidey mask up above his eyes to get a better look at its controls.

As the pressure built up inside it with nowhere to go, the battery bounced up and down off the ground. Peter looked at the tangle of wires on its control panel in utter confusion. He tried to remember the drawings from Octavius' apartment, hoping he could figure out how to shut it down. But between his danger sense and the alarming buzz from the battery, Peter couldn't concentrate. He thought about ripping all the wires out of it — but remembering Octavius' history of lab accidents, he knew that wouldn't be a good idea.

But as his head pounded in pain, he remembered...his danger-sense! He had trusted it against Octavius, and it had worked. If he was going to pull out the wrong wire, perhaps it would warn him. But it would take

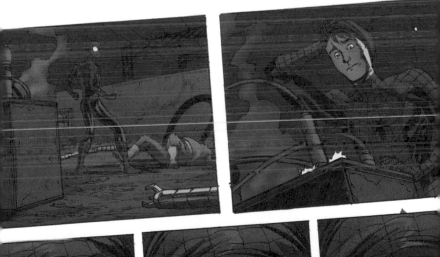

a lot of concentration. He looked at the control panel again and saw three main wires: red, yellow and green. Peter traced the red wire with his finger. The battery was so loud now, he couldn't hear himself think — but his danger sense was quiet. He traced his finger along the yellow wire — no change there, either. But when he moved his hand to the green wire, his danger sense rang so loudly, it rattled his teeth! The battery sparked. The contacts began to smoke. He would have to be crazy to trust the fate of New York City to this strange "spider-sense," wouldn't he? This was a matter of life and death! But Peter had no choice. It was now or never. He gripped the green wire between his fingers and squeezed his eyes shut. If there was ever a time he needed any luck, it was at that moment. Then, in one quick motion, like peeling off a band-aid, he snapped his wrist and —

Everything went silent. The battery's buzz, his spider-sense — everything. Peter lifted his eyelids one at a time and saw the battery lying cold and lifeless, except for the spray of steam slowly escaping from its seams. The city was saved!

Peter fell onto his back and thought about what a crazy day it had

been. Just a few weeks ago, his biggest problem in the world had been Flash Thompson and the bullies at Midtown High; now, he was saving New York City from a nuclear explosion caused by a guy that looked like an octopus. The more he thought about it, the more ridiculous it seemed. It started with a smile, his first one in a long time, and then a familiar feeling slowly bubbled in his gut. It came out as a chuckle at first, but in a few short seconds grew into a laugh — and before long he howled loudly into the night sky.

By the time Peter got back to the apartment, Aunt May had already gone to bed. His body was so tired he could have fallen asleep the minute his head touched the pillow, but a delicious scent coming from the kitchen called to him. He hadn't eaten all day, so he followed his nose all the way to a place setting at his regular seat at the table where a big bowl of beef stew was waiting for him. Peter slapped his forehead! He had forgotten all about the special dinner Aunt May had planned for them. Even though she'd had every right to throw the food away, she didn't. Instead, she had left it there for him to enjoy when he was ready, however long that took. She knew that people dealt with things in different ways, and that Peter would eventually come to her with the truth.

As he ate, he realized doing the right thing didn't always feel good. In fact, a lot of times, it felt pretty lousy. But he didn't risk his life to help

others because he wanted to. He did it because he *had* to. He knew he was much stronger and faster than any police officer. If he hadn't helped, there was no one else who could have stopped Octavius. He felt badly for hurting Aunt May's feelings, but he could never forget Uncle Ben's lesson: with great power comes great responsibility. In the morning he'd make up an excuse, apologize to Aunt May and sit down with her for a proper family breakfast. It was long overdue.

Ben Urich of *The Daily Bugle* was the only reporter in the city who had covered the story of how Spider-Man saved all of their lives from the terrible explosion. In spite of Jonah's headline calling Spider-Man a "menace," Peter couldn't help but smile.

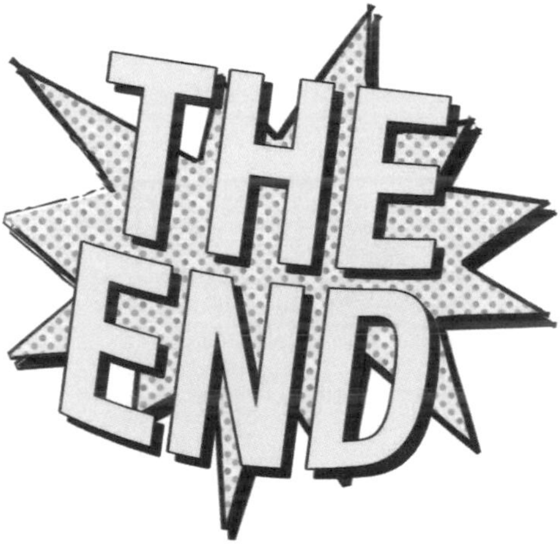
THE END